READ
THE BIBLE
FOR THE
FIRST TIME

Diane Woerner

Segen Press
Arrington, Tennessee 37014

ISBN: 978-0-578-01088-5

To order copies, contact:
  Segen Press
  P.O. Box 333
  Arrington, TN 37014
  www.segenpress.com

Printed in the United States of America
by Bethany Press International.

I rejoice at Your word,
as one who finds great treasure.

Psalm 119:162

Preface

Dear Bible Reader,

I'm so excited!

In the first place, I'm excited because there's a good chance that the reason you have this little book is because you have recently chosen to say yes to Jesus, and now the God of the universe, by His Holy Spirit, has made you really alive in your spirit. Welcome to the family of God!

It's possible, of course, that you haven't yet made the decision to trust God with your life. In that case, you may be wanting to read the Bible so you can see for yourself if what it teaches about God might really be true. But that's also exciting! Many people have joined God's family because of what they learned about Him in the pages of His book.

The third possibility is that you have been in God's family for quite a while, but for some reason you have had a hard time understanding the Bible. Don't feel badly about that. It's a large and unusual book, and there are a lot of reasons why it isn't exactly easy to read.

But whatever your reason is for being a Bible beginner, I can promise you one thing. Next to your decision to make Jesus the ruler of your life, the second most important decision you can make is to open His wonderful book and begin a lifetime journey of finding out as much as you can about what God has revealed about Himself, about you, and about His plans for all of us.

I've divided this instruction book into three parts. The first part provides some basic information about the Bible that you should know before you begin to read it. The second part contains short descriptions of what is actually IN the Bible. Part three will show you some ways to gain even more from what you read. It concludes with a summary of the Bible's most important message.

It is my prayer that God will truly meet you in the pages of His Word. I also pray that you'll find the wisdom and encouragement you need to grow in faith and to please Him. Finally, as you continue over the next months and years to explore the most fascinating book ever written, I pray that God will teach you how to pass along what you learn to others, so they too will become hungry for the "Bread of Life," Jesus Christ.

In His love,

Diane Woerner

Table of Contents

PART ONE

Things You'll Need to Know

The Bible is a Miracle!

When you made your decision to begin reading the Bible, you may not know that you're opening up the number one best selling book in all of human history. In fact, the man who invented the printing press, back in the 1400's, did so because he wanted to be able to print copies of the Bible so more people could read it. Even before that, people sometimes spent their entire lives carefully hand-copying the Bible so its message wouldn't be lost. In countries where the Bible has been declared illegal to read, it quickly becomes one of the most precious possessions many people have.

What makes the Bible so valuable? Why doesn't it ever get outdated? Why hasn't any other history book, or novel, or moral instruction book, ever gotten close to being this popular?

The answer is simply that the Bible is a miracle. It is a supernatural book. It was written because the God who created you and me decided He wanted to teach us about Himself and His plans by having people write certain things down – stories and ideas and songs and letters. Together, these writings (also called "scriptures") have communicated to all of humanity throughout all of history the specific things that God desires us to understand.

You may already know that the Bible (unlike most books) was written by many authors over hundreds of years of time. Some of these authors had no way of reading what the other authors were writing. Yet, miraculously, the Bible is internally consistent. By that I mean it doesn't disagree with itself, especially not about important things. The God about whom these different authors wrote has the same personality and the same requirements and the same goals, from one end of the Bible to the other.

How was the Bible actually written? Experts have argued about this for many years, but in truth, no one really knows for sure. Some parts of the Bible are letters, and in these the writer usually identifies himself. Other parts are written as history or as poetry, and again, the author sometimes mentions who he is. In the case of some of the oldest Bible stories, it is assumed that they were passed on from generation to generation by story-tellers. But this still doesn't really tell us who finally wrote the stories down, or why.

Perhaps an even greater mystery is how these writers were able to record conversations and speeches that happened when no one was taking notes. In our world of recorders and cameras, we sometimes forget that for most of human history, no one even carried a notepad and pencil around. Some parts of the Bible are private prayers – who would have written them down? The story of Job opens with a conversation in heaven between God and Satan. Who was there listening to them? The very beginning of the Bible tells how God created the world out of nothing. There surely weren't any human eye witnesses during *that* event.

This brings us to a very important decision that you must make before you begin to read the Bible. Because so much of what is written is humanly impossible to know, either we must conclude that it came out of someone's imagination – or – we must believe that God's Spirit supernaturally directed what these writers said.

If you decide the Bible is just the work of some brilliant ancient thinkers, it becomes a little hard to explain why it has been so honored and treasured throughout history. Lots of other truly brilliant writers haven't had their books sell anywhere near this well.

But more significantly, once you decide that even part of the Bible might just be the result of someone's clever thinking, you lose out on its most important benefit, which comes from its claim to be God's personal communication to us.

You see, those of us who have learned to passionately love this book love it because it can be *trusted*. We can "put our weight" on it. For us, it defines what is true and good. As we'll discuss a little later, there is a lot in the Bible that isn't exactly clear and straightforward. Certain ideas have produced some significant arguments among believers throughout the centuries.

But underneath the confusion lies a unified faith that God deliberately chose what was written. We believe that not only did God inspire Biblical writings, He also directed the men in the early church who gathered the texts together to create the first complete Bible. Further, we believe He has protected the Bible's accuracy when it was hand-copied or printed over the centuries.

If you can agree with us that the Bible is a supernatural writing which is trustworthy and which carries God's authority in its pages, then you are in a place where you can take the final and most important step. You see, just as the Spirit of God miraculously guided all of those writers in the distant past, *His Spirit is also able to guide us today as we read His Word.*

It's really quite amazing and wonderful. Even if you're not an especially good reader, and you find yourself stumbling over a lot of what you'll find written in the Bible, somehow God is able to bring those ancient words to life in a way that will change you forever. (On the other hand, there are some highly educated scholars who find the Bible dry and boring, because they don't understand what it really is, and they also don't know about their need to have the Spirit's help when they read it.)

So, as you open the pages of your Bible, also open your mind and heart to hear God. Ask Him to teach you. Ask Him for answers to some of the questions that are troubling you in your life. Ask Him to show you the places inside you where your fears or rebelliousness might be keeping you from knowing Him better.

If you'll do this, you'll begin to understand that reading the Bible isn't some duty we must do because God is strict and demanding. It's also not a matter of learning all the rules so we can live a perfect life.

Instead, it's God's chosen way of having a living relationship with us here on earth, before we meet Him in person in heaven. It's like His letter written to us per-

6

sonally. Even though the Bible was written years ago by people we never met, it was also written by our Father who knew even back then who we would be and what we would need to know.

How He manages to fit those old words into my modern life I have no idea – but He really does it! I've read the Bible many times, and somehow there is always something new and astonishing and intensely personal to be found in it, each time God and I meet over those pages. And so I welcome you to this adventure. Join with me and millions of others as we read together the book that God wrote.

What's In the Bible?

While some of you may already know something about how the Bible is put together, others may not. This chapter is designed to introduce you to the parts of the Bible so you'll be able to make your way around it without getting lost.

The Bible is divided into two main sections, called the Old Testament and the New Testament. The Old Testament is roughly three times as long as the New Testament, and it includes writings from the beginning of history up until a few hundred years before Jesus was born. The New Testament tells the story of the life of Jesus, and also contains the writings of some of His followers after He returned to heaven.

The Bible is made up of 66 books, 39 in the Old Testament and 27 in the New Testament. Some of the books are named after the man who wrote them, and others are named for what they contain.

Eventually it would be helpful to memorize the names of these books, so you can find passages more quickly. However, your Bible has a table of contents in the front, and also the name of each book is printed at the top of the page to help you as well. Most people soon learn how to find their favorite books, once they've begun exploring their Bible.

Somewhere back in time someone also decided to divide each book into chapters, and then to further divide each chapter into verses. A verse will usually have only a sentence or two in it. In fact, it's common for a long sentence to stretch out across several verses. This system makes it easy to identify exactly where something is written, and it is a great help for memorizing scripture portions that are especially valuable.

Thus, when you see a scripture reference written like this – James 1:5 – it means the fifth verse in the first chapter of the book of James (which you'll find near the end of the New Testament). In a few cases there are two books with the same name, such as I Kings and II Kings (we say First Kings and Second Kings), and in the New Testament there are four books with the name "John": the gospel of John (his version of the life of Jesus) and three of his letters (I John, II John, and III John). But you'll catch on to all this pretty quickly, I'm sure.

In Part Two of this book I have included brief descriptions of each book of the Bible, so you'll have an idea what's in them. For now, I'd like to tell you about the general types of books that can be found in the Old and New Testaments.

The first half of the Old Testament is made up of history books, with a few story-books scattered in. A leader named Moses wrote the first five books, beginning with the creation story found in Genesis, and continuing through the journey of the Israelites out of Egypt. Then other historians record the reigns of various kings, telling of battles and other events in the lives of those ancient people. Throughout these stories, however, you will find God calling His chosen nation (the Israelites) to obey Him, and you will also see that whenever they disobeyed, He would take drastic measures to draw their attention back to Him.

If you open most Bibles right in the middle, you will find yourself in the book of Psalms. (Some Bibles have extra notes written around the scriptures, which might throw things off a bit.) Psalms is the longest book in the Bible, and it contains poetry and worship songs composed by a king named David and other writers. Right after Psalms is a book called Proverbs, which contains little nuggets of wisdom written or collected by David's son Solomon. Solomon also wrote two other shorter books that come after Proverbs.

The final section of the Old Testament contains a series of books written by (and named after) prophets. While a few of these books include some great stories, they are primarily warnings to God's people of judgments He would bring to them for their rebellion and disobedience.

As you read these prophetic books, however, you will also discover some wonderful promises woven in between the warnings. Many of these promises were not only for the people who lived in those days, but are also promises for us today. In addition, you will find some fascinating verses that predict what would happen during Jesus' time on earth, prophecies that the New Testament writers refer back to as they tell the story of His life.

The New Testament opens with four different versions of the life of Jesus Christ, known as the four gospels. Each writer (Matthew, Mark, Luke and John) tells the story from a different perspective. Some events and sermons are in only one book, while others show up in three or four of them. These are probably the most important books in your Bible, and most people begin their Bible reading with them. We'll talk more about that in our next chapter.

Following the gospels, Luke writes a sequel called "The Acts of the Apostles," which is usually shortened to just "Acts." Apostles were men who carried the message of Jesus and the salvation He offered to people in many countries who didn't know about Him. These were also the men who founded the first Christian churches.

All but one of the remaining books in the New Testament are letters written by the early church leaders. An apostle named Paul writes most of them, and these books are named after the towns or people to whom he was writing. Some letters are written by other men, and they are named after the writers. All of the New Testament letters (which are sometimes called "epistles") are filled with useful instructions to believers in every century. Through the wisdom the Spirit gave these men, we are able to learn how to live as Christians, how to avoid sin and deception, and how to serve each other in obedience to God.

The very last book in the Bible is called "Revelation." It is actually the fifth book written by John, who was one of Jesus' closest friends. Revelation describes an astonishing vision that John saw near the end of his life. Even though it is filled with symbols that are not easy to understand, it is apparent that God wanted to give us, as the grand finale of His book, some insight into what will happen when He decides to end this part of human history, just before Jesus returns to earth to become the ruler of everything.

How to Read Your Bible

One of the wonderful things about the Bible is that there isn't just one right way to read it. With most books, you start at the front and read to the end. But the Bible is more like a huge plate filled with different kinds of food. You can eat whatever you like first! It's all good, and it all has something valuable to give you.

Nevertheless, I will tell you that some parts of the Bible are a little easier to digest than others, especially for beginners. If you know absolutely nothing about what's in the Bible, it would probably be best to begin with the story of the life of Jesus. But as I mentioned earlier, even here you have four choices to pick from: Matthew, Mark, Luke or John. Many people believe Mark is the easiest one to start with.

Everything else in the Bible either points forward to Jesus, or refers back to Him. So you'll need to know about the miracle of His birth, the amazing powers He had during His three years of ministry, and the divine wisdom of His teachings. More importantly, you need to learn about His obedience to His Father, when God allowed wicked men to kill His Son so that through His horrible death He could take the punishment we deserved. You also need to read for yourself the glory of His victory over death, when God brought Jesus back to life and thereby proved He can give each of us eternal life as well. It is truly the greatest story ever told.

After you have gotten acquainted with the details of Jesus' life, death, and resurrection, how you read the Bible depends on what kind of person you are. Let me describe a few kinds of "reading personalities" – maybe one of these will fit you!

1. The builder

This kind of person likes to do things systematically. He wants to lay a foundation, and not miss any of the details. A builder would probably be most comfortable if he went back to the beginning of the Bible, and started with the creation story. He would then work through the history of Noah, Abraham, Joseph, Moses, David, and other heroes of the Bible.

After he's done with those beginning books (say, through II Kings), he may decide to move ahead and learn about the history of the early church. He might re-read one or more of the gospels (it never hurts to read those often!), and then continue on through Acts. By this time he would have a pretty good idea of the "who, when and where" of the Bible. To this framework he could eventually attach other pieces of scripture, fitting them together as he discovers the beauty of God's architectural masterpiece.

Some Bibles give extra assistance to folks who like to see the whole picture. Often a Bible will have maps in the back that show where the countries were located during the different periods of history. Other Bibles provide time-lines and other charts that give the dates when people lived and when various events took place. Check out these tools if you have them.

2. The explorer

This style of reader likes to plunge into things for the sheer adventure of it. He wants to sample a little of everything on the plate. Having gotten his bearings from the gospels, he might decide to read some Old Testament stories, then maybe check out some poetry in the Psalms or some of the wisdom of Proverbs. Or he may choose to look over the letters of Paul, or even see what Revelation is about.

There's nothing wrong with this, because God can be found throughout the entire Bible. If this is your style, however, I would encourage you to move slowly enough, wherever you read, to allow His Spirit to speak to you. Also, when you begin to discover the many treasures that are buried in those pages, make yourself a map! Do some underlining, put notes in the margins, or perhaps write things down on the blank pages at the back of your Bible (or in a special notebook), so you can get back to your treasures again.

Many Bibles have tools to help readers who want to look for particular subjects. Check to see if your Bible has a "concordance," which is an alphabetical listing of certain words that are found in Bible verses. Maybe you want to read about Daniel, or perhaps you want to know which verses speak of heaven. If so, this would be a good tool to use. Your concordance won't list every verse or every word, but it does include many of the most important ones.

3. *The gourmet*

This reader moves slowly, carefully tasting and enjoying each item on his plate. He isn't in a hurry to know everything, but he definitely wants to understand what he is reading about. He wants to know why a passage was written, what it reveals about the nature of God, and what it has to do with his own life. He compares the struggles of Bible characters to the challenges he faces, and desires to benefit from the lessons they learned.

After thoroughly digesting one or more of the gospels, this kind of person might be happiest going next to some of the teaching scriptures. In the Old Testament those would include Psalms and Proverbs, or Isaiah and Jeremiah. In the New Testament, he could spend months examining the letters of Paul and the other church leaders (Romans would be a perfect place to start).

One thing that could be very valuable to this kind of reader is what are called "cross references." If your Bible has these, they're located in the margins beside or between the columns of verses. If you find something that interests you in verse 7 of the chapter you're on, look for a "7" in the cross reference column. There you'll find some other verses listed in other parts of the Bible that discuss the same ideas.

Whatever type of reader you are, the most important thing is for you to find a method that keeps you going back. Some people try to read the Bible all the way through in a year. If that works for you, fine! But for many of us, a slower pace is better and less likely to be discouraging. A check-off chart can be too much like a school-teacher, putting pressure on you that doesn't really need to be there.

On the other hand, it is going to take some effort to really focus on what you're reading. Many people these days are used to things being fast and flashy. Bible study requires quiet, steady, persistent attention. But gradually, as you are able to meditate on and memorize those special verses where God has spoken most clearly to you personally, you will find you have gained treasures that will last a lifetime.

Getting Over the Bumps

Like most things in life that are worth anything, reading your Bible can sometimes be challenging. Even people who have been reading the Bible for years still run into difficulties. In this section I'd like to talk about a few problems you might encounter, and then give you some suggestions on how to work through them.

The first and biggest problem for some of you may just be the words themselves. Maybe you aren't much of a reader, and the language seems to be so very complicated. One thing you should know is that there are a number of translations of the Bible available today. The original writers used Hebrew (in the Old Testament) and Greek (in the New Testament), so you are reading someone else's translation of those languages into English.

For several centuries, most English Bibles were published in the "King James Version." This translation used words that are rather unfamiliar to us (words like "thee," "thou" and "ye" instead of "you," "hast" instead of "have," and so forth). If for some reason this is the only version of the Bible you have available, you may need a little extra patience until you get used to the style. But most of the words will still be ones you can understand, and it won't be long before you'll stop noticing those that are old-fashioned.

Many of you will be able to find a more modern translation that will make things easier for you. Three of the more popular translations today are the New International Version (NIV), the New King James Version (NKJV), and the New American Standard version (NAS). You'll probably see one of these printed on the outside cover of your Bible. While each one will translate the scriptures a little differently, they all try hard to change the original Greek and Hebrew words into English words that mean exactly the same thing. They understand how important it is to keep God's message accurate.

There is also, however, another kind of Bible that has become more common these days called a "paraphrase." With these, the authors are not simply translating the words, but rather are attempting to put the ideas of the Bible into a more modern form of expression. Two quite popular paraphrases of the Bible are *The Living Bible* and *The Message*. If you happen to have one of these, you'll probably find that it's quite easy to understand and even fun to read.

However, because these Bibles are interpretations instead of translations, they may not really be the best kind of Bible for you to start with. It isn't that the authors are not godly people; it's simply that whenever you mix human understandings into scripture, it opens up the possibility that their ideas might not be exactly what God meant to say.

We mentioned earlier that one of the wonderful things about the Bible is that it is intended to carry authority. Its words are meant by God to be something we can "put our weight on" with regard to our moral decisions and other aspects of living. Paraphrases can be helpful in suggesting possible insights we may not have thought of ourselves, but that's somewhat different than what the Bible claims to be, which is the written-down words of God. For this reason, they shouldn't be trusted as much.

Let's move on to another possible problem area. Let's say you have decided to read your Bible by starting at the front cover and working straight through to the back. For quite a while you'll do fine, because in the early part of the scriptures there are lots of really fascinating stories. But eventually you'll run into some things that might seem boring, like long lists of families with strange names, or what appear to be picky details about how the Israelites were supposed to build the tabernacle.

It would help at these points to remember again that you aren't in school and you aren't going to be tested on how much of those passages you can understand and remember. While God had His own definite reasons for what He chose to put in the Bible, some of these may not be important to you right away. What is important, however, is that you don't stop reading. No one will judge you if you skim ahead until you find something that makes more sense.

This brings us to what is probably the most common struggle that all of us face, which is that Bible reading isn't always what we want to do. Part of it is due to our own human laziness. We must also remember, however, that we have a real spiritual enemy who doesn't want us to know what God has said. Satan's biggest weapons are lies, and he is very aware that our understanding of God's truth can break the confusion and deceptions which he uses to keep us from growing spiritually.

Just as soldiers and athletes get into shape by working out even when they're tired and sore, so Christians must be willing to do things that aren't easy in order to build spiritual muscles. It's called discipline. Two of the most important disciplines for Christians are prayer and Bible reading. A third one that's also important is getting together regularly with other believers to challenge and encourage each other.

I would suggest a simple plan. Promise yourself that at least once a day you'll open your Bible and read at least five or ten verses. Then either before or after you read, spend at least a few minutes talking to God. There may be some days when you can read many chapters, or spend an hour or more in prayer. That would be wonderful! But if you can't, you'll still be developing a habit that in the long run will make a surprising difference in your spiritual health.

It's also okay to stall out on one passage of scripture and read it over and over. An amazing thing about the Word of God is how deeply you can dig into it, and still not run out of new things to discover. Remember, Bible reading is different than any other kind of reading, because God has promised that as we study His words, His Spirit in us will teach us what He wants us to know.

One final "bump" needs to be mentioned. At some point as you're reading through your Bible, you're going to come across some situations or ideas that will upset you. For example, you won't read very far in the Old Testament before you'll realize that God Himself was responsible for killing many thousands of people. Or in the New Testament, you'll find that most of the writers (and even Jesus Himself) talk about pain and suffering as a blessing. Then there are the commands of Jesus that tell us to do a lot of things that seem pretty ridiculous, like loving our enemies, or giving our coat to someone just because they ask us for it.

We live in a world where we buy things based on how attractive or pleasing they are to us. Advertisers make promises that their products will be wonderful and safe and easy to use. The Bible is different. It wasn't written based on what we might want to read; it was written based on what God wanted to say. It's *His* book. And He purposely decided to make quite a lot of it challenging to us.

Even those of us who have been reading the Bible for many years can't explain all the hard parts to you. Some portions of scripture contain mysteries that won't be solved until we get to heaven. But what we *can* tell you is that in spite of our questions, we have personally discovered the God of the Bible to be wonderfully loving and powerful and good. As we have learned to be humble (not demanding answers for everything), His Spirit has poured into our spirits an ability to trust Him, to believe that He has a kind of wisdom that is simply higher than ours.

And over the years, it does begin to make sense, in a way that those who don't know God probably could never understand. As I said earlier, the Bible isn't a book of rules or even a philosophy book. Rather, it's a letter from God to us. The reason we get excited about any letter we receive has nothing to do with the paper and ink, or even the fancy words. It's because we care about the person who wrote it, and we really want to know what they have to say to us.

So as you begin your adventure with God and His word, I would encourage you to relax – to be patient with yourself – and to realize that God wants you not only to understand what you read, but even more He wants you to find Him. In fact, let's start now! See if you can locate the book of Jeremiah (it's a little to the right of Psalms, just past Isaiah). Find chapter 9, and then find verses 23 and 24. Here in just two small verses, you will find a summary of what really matters to God.

PART TWO

The Books
of the Bible

Introduction

I hope by now that you're beginning to get a lot more interested in the best book ever written. In this section you will find a short description of each book in the Bible. I would suggest that you read through these summaries from start to finish – it really won't take very long!

What will happen then is that when you finally start reading your actual Bible, it will feel somewhat familiar, like a person you're meeting for the second time, or a town you've visited before. It also helps to understand the historical places and events that are the context for these scriptures, and to be aware of some of the things that are known about the authors themselves.

In addition, the summaries will assist you in choosing where to begin your reading. You might make some notes as you go along, when certain books sound especially worth checking out. Feel free to keep this book handy, too, when you begin your exploration of the Bible. Something I've written just might help you make sense of some of the more confusing portions of scripture.

But most importantly, remember to make it a habit to ask God's Spirit to explain things you don't understand. He wants you to understand and accept His truths even more than you do. Those of us who read the Bible regularly have all had that wonderful experience when a verse suddenly "comes to life," and we know God Himself has spoken to us personally through His word. I pray this will happen for you as well.

The Old Testament Books

Genesis (beginnings)

Genesis is a wonderful series of stories, starting with the creation of the world, the creation of Adam and Eve, and their falling away from God. It tells of God's decision to keep the human race alive because one man (Noah) is still faithful to Him. God later finds another faithful man, Abraham, and promises in a covenant to make his family line (through his son Isaac and grandson Jacob, later renamed Israel) into a nation that will belong to Him in a unique way. He also tells Abraham that one of his descendants will one day become a blessing to all the nations of the earth. Genesis ends with the story of Jacob's son Joseph, which demonstrates how situations which start out as evil can be used by God for great good.

Exodus (a journey out)

Exodus opens with the Israelites becoming slaves in Egypt. This time God chooses a baby named Moses, who, after many years and some important lessons, is called to lead God's people out of their slavery. In the process, God is able to demonstrate His supernatural powers to the Egyptian ruler Pharaoh, and to us. God promises the Israelites that He will take them to a new land full of great blessing. While they are on their long, difficult journey from Egypt to the land of promise, God gives them many instructions, including the Ten Commandments. He also has them build Him a tent, called the tabernacle, that is designed to be moved as the Israelites travel. It is a special place where men who have properly prepared themselves can meet with Him.

Leviticus (things pertaining to the Levites)

The Levites (sons of Levi, who was another one of Jacob's twelve sons) are selected by God to be the priests of Israel. While you'll find a few stories in this book, most of it is a discussion of the rituals and laws that God gives Israel to test their loyalty and willingness to be obedient. The rituals include a series of offerings that help us see the significance of sacrifices in God's system, so we can better understand the eventual sacrifice of His Son. Many of the laws are related to things like cleanliness and good eating. Some of the laws however will surprise you, and may seem harsh or strange. These were God's way of demonstrating the severe nature of His holiness. In the end, the Israelites are not willing to keep the laws, proving that they (and we) are not able to gain holiness in any other way except through the salvation of Jesus.

Numbers

Numbers continues the story of the Israelites (who are also known as Jews) and their journey toward their promised land. The book gets its name from a census that is taken of the Israelite tribes. (By the way, the nation of Israel is divided into twelve tribes, named after the twelve sons of Jacob. The exception to this is when God makes the Levites into priests, they are treated differently from the other tribes. God then makes two tribes from Joseph's sons, Ephraim and Manasseh.) Numbers also contains many stories, and more detailed instructions, laws, and rituals. It is in this book that we meet Joshua, who will become Israel's next leader.

Deuteronomy (a review of the law, literally "second law")

Deuteronomy contains a series of sermons Moses gives to the Israelites just before he dies. He begins by reminiscing about their long journey through the wilderness, and reminds the people of the many things God has done for them. He then restates the Ten Commandments and many of the other laws. He concludes by emphasizing God's promise of great blessings if the people will only obey Him, and His frightening curses if they choose to disobey.

Joshua

After Moses dies, Joshua finally leads the people into the promised land, Canaan. Even though God is giving the Israelites this pleasant new homeland, there is still the matter of removing the tribes that currently live there. These are sinful, idol-worshipping people with whom God is not pleased. Joshua's first battle, at Jericho, is won by the supernatural power of God in response to the Israelites' obedience. Their second battle, however, doesn't go as well. But eventually the land is won, and is divided among the twelve tribes according to God's instructions.

Judges

Unfortunately, it doesn't take long for the Israelites to forget their God, and they begin to worship some of the other gods in their new land. This brings upon them some of the punishments they were warned would take place. However, God doesn't abandon them. Instead He raises up judges, men (and one woman) who are filled with His Spirit and who help deliver the people from their enemies each time they repent.

Ruth

After all the wars and bloodshed, Ruth is a refreshing story about a young woman who is not an Israelite, but who chooses to be loyal to her Israelite mother-in-law, Naomi, and the God Naomi serves. You will enjoy reading about the rewards she is given for her humble service and her obedient trust.

I Samuel

Along with Genesis, First Samuel is one of the best story-books in the Old Testament. One of the main characters in these stories is a prophet named Samuel, whom God raises up after the priests become too corrupt to lead the people. But at the insistence of the people, God allows Samuel to appoint a real king, Saul –

who starts strong but doesn't end up doing so well. We also meet a young shepherd named David, who will eventually replace Saul as king.

II Samuel

Maybe this book should have been called Second David, since Samuel actually dies in the first book. Even though David is one of the most famous men in all the Bible, and even though he is (for the most part) faithful to God, the story of his reign is filled with wars and pain. Besides being a king, David is also a musician and a poet, and out of his struggles and heartache come some of the most beautiful and inspiring writings in scripture.

I Kings

After David's death, his son Solomon becomes king. This is another story of a king who starts well and ends poorly. But in between that beginning and end, Solomon is permitted to build a more permanent home for God in Jerusalem (Israel's main city), a beautiful temple that replaces the tabernacle. When Solomon dies, there is a struggle for power that ends up dividing the kingdom. From then on, the tribes in the northern part of the land keep the name Israel, while those in the south (an area which includes Jerusalem) are called Judah. A series of kings (mostly bad ones) rule the two new kingdoms. So God chooses another prophet named Elijah to confront one of the kings, Ahab, who is particularly wicked.

II Kings

The stories of these kings serve as a background for some of the most amazing miracles in the Old Testament, performed by Elijah and then by his student Elisha. But eventually Elisha dies, and the two kingdoms grow weaker and more vulnerable to their enemies. One of the strongest of these enemies is Assyria. Because of the continued sinfulness of His people, God allows Assyria to conquer Israel. Many years later, most of the people of Judah are also carried away to a country called Babylon.

I and II Chronicles (historical records)

The people from the northern kingdom of Israel never returned to their homeland. But after seventy years of exile (captivity) in Babylon, the people of Judah are allowed to return and rebuild their temple in Jerusalem. The books of I and II Chronicles were written after they returned, to remind the people of their history and their heritage. For this reason, much of what you will find in these books repeats the stories from I and II Kings.

Ezra

God had promised the people of Judah before they were taken to Babylon that they wouldn't be there forever. True to His promise, He "stirred up the spirit" of the king of Babylon, who sends a group of exiles back to Jerusalem to begin rebuilding the temple, which had been destroyed. One of these men is a priest named

Ezra, who is also a scribe (a writer). This book is his record of their return and the challenges the people faced.

Nehemiah (pronounced nee-uh-my-uh)

After the temple is restored the people begin to rebuild the walls of the city of Jerusalem, but they soon get discouraged. This time God stirs the heart of a man named Nehemiah, who is the cupbearer for the king in Babylon. After getting permission to journey to Jerusalem, Nehemiah persuades the Jewish people who are already there to finish the walls in spite of some difficult opposition. Nehemiah is an excellent example of God's kind of leadership.

Esther (pronounced ess-ter)

This wonderful story tells about a Jewish woman named Esther who, while exiled in Babylon, is faithful to God and obedient to those in authority over her. Other characters include her humble cousin Mordecai, the powerful king Ahasuerus, and a wicked man named Haman. It's an adventure filled with suspense and plot twists, but finally God's victory in a desperate situation was so impressive that it is celebrated by the Jews even to this day.

Job (pronounced jobe)

Job is one of the more mysterious books of the Bible in that we don't know who wrote it or when the story takes place. Job is a good man minding his own business when God and Satan decide to test his faithfulness by putting him through some devastating trials. Even his best friends can't understand what is happening, and assume Job has committed some terrible sin. They have long discussions trying to figure out a reason for all his sufferings. In the end, God points out that He knows more than Job, and thus Job and his friends (and we) are wrong when we question what He does.

Psalms (pronounced sahlms)

What might be called the heart of the Bible, Psalms is filled with praise and wisdom. It contains poems and song lyrics, many of which were used in worship. Other psalms are the deeply emotional prayers of writers such as king David, containing fear and regrets as well as rejoicing and adoration. There is a lot to be discovered in this book, including some very specific prophecies about the life, death, and resurrection of Jesus. When the New Testament writers quote the Old Testament, about half the time they are quoting something from Psalms.

Proverbs

God once asked king Solomon what gift he would like, and when Solomon asked for wisdom, God promised to make him the wisest man who ever lived. Proverbs is a collection of wise sayings that Solomon either wrote or collected from other wise thinkers. You will find frequent contrasts between men and women who are wise and hardworking and moral, and those who are foolish or lazy or wicked. Because Proverbs has 31 chapters, some people read one for each day of the month. But you might need to move more slowly – there's a LOT to think about!

Ecclesiastes (one who is speaking to a group)

Even though Solomon was given great wisdom, he did not always live by it. By the end of his life he had made some serious mistakes. Through them he learned that wisdom – along with great power, impressive accomplishments, and enormous wealth – did not end up making him truly happy. The theme of this book is the meaninglessness of life (some translations use the word "vanity"). However, while nothing seems worthwhile "under the sun," Solomon admits there are things of value to be found in a right relationship with God.

Song of Solomon

This unusual little book celebrates the glory of love, both physical love and (symbolically) the love of God for His people. Written in the form of a play, with rich, colorful language, it demonstrates God's blessing on the sexual pleasures of a man and woman who are committed to one another in marriage. It also contains a warning not to "awaken love until it pleases." In other words, sexual feelings are not to be deliberately stirred up until the proper time.

Isaiah (pronounced eye-zay-uh)

The prophetic section of the Old Testament opens with what is probably the strongest of these books. Isaiah writes his prophetic warnings to the northern kingdom (Israel) and the southern kingdom (Judah) before they were taken into exile. He specifically identifies many of their sins and reminds them of God's promised curses on disobedience. The amazing thing about Isaiah, however, is that scattered throughout these very dark passages are some of the Bible's brightest promises, both for Israel and for the church Jesus will eventually raise up. You will also discover detailed descriptions of how Jesus will be born, how and why He will have to die, and what the future will hold after His resurrection.

Jeremiah (pronounced jehr-uh-my-uh)

Jeremiah gives us an interesting look at the personal life of an Old Testament prophet, and it certainly isn't pleasant! His consistent warnings of the coming judgments make him very unpopular with nearly everyone. His life is threatened, he is imprisoned several times, and once he is thrown into a dungeon where he sinks down into the mud. Yet God always sustains him, and Jeremiah continues to speak God's words faithfully. Between his frightening descriptions of disaster are messages of hope, indicating not only that God will one day restore the kingdom, but also that the nations who are oppressing God's people will themselves be overthrown.

Lamentations (mournings)

It is believed that Jeremiah also wrote this little book, not so much as a prophetic warning as a deep grieving over what he knows will soon be happening to his nation. In a series of Hebrew poems, he paints a vivid picture of the sorrows that are to come. At the same time, he is communicating an important message. The suffering of the people, severe as it will be, is designed by God to draw them back to Himself, to bring them to a place where they can rediscover His faithfulness and goodness.

Ezekiel (pronounced ee-zeke-ee-el)

Unlike Isaiah and Jeremiah, who are speaking of future events, Ezekiel is actually taken into Babylonian captivity with one of the groups of exiles. His ministry begins a few years later with a series of remarkable visions, after which God tells him to make it clear to the people of Judah that He is punishing their nation for its sins. This includes some rather strange "role playing" to symbolize God's messages. But Ezekiel encourages the people to turn back to God as individuals, and to learn to live in their new home as peacefully as they can. One day, he tells them, God will allow them to return to Jerusalem, and will punish the heathen people who have oppressed them.

Daniel

Daniel opens with several fascinating stories about a group of young men from Judah who are chosen to be servants of the Babylonian king. Their decision to remain devoted to the God of Israel in the middle of a heathen court gets them into some extremely frightening situations! God also gives Daniel very unusual prophetic abilities, and later in the book you will find his strange dreams about the future, some of which symbolically describe the end of human history. He also speaks of the Messiah (which means anointed one), whom the Jews believe will one day come to save their nation.

Hosea (pronounced hoe-zay-uh)

God uses many different methods to explain to His people how He views their relationship with Him. Hosea is told to find a prostitute and to marry her, representing God's commitment to a nation that is not worthy of His love. When Hosea's wife leaves him (just as God's people have turned against Him), God tells Hosea to find her and take her back. In the same way, God is willing to pay the price to redeem (buy back) His people who have sinned.

Joel (pronounced jole)

In yet a different kind of prophecy, Joel explains the meaning of a severe natural disaster that has come upon the land of Judah many years prior to their exile. For some reason, an enormous swarm of locusts (grasshoppers) has completely eaten all the plants in the region, which means there is no food for the people or their animals. This is one of the punishments for sin God had spoken of back in the book of Deuteronomy. In part Joel is calling the people of Judah to repent, but also he is warning us about the judgments that will come at the end of time.

Amos (pronounced ā-mus)

Also written many years before the exile, Amos directs his prophecies primarily to the northern kingdom of Israel. The nation is prospering economically and politically, so they believe God is blessing them. But Amos points out their immorality, their oppression of the poor, and the corruption of their legal system. God then gives him a series of visions that tell of coming disasters.

Obadiah (pronounced oh-buh-die-uh)

In a change of pace, Obadiah's prophecies are directed toward an enemy of the Israelites, the nation of Edom. These people are the descendants of Jacob's twin brother Esau and live southeast of Judah. When the Babylonian armies start attacking Judah, the

Edomites join them and help to overthrow Jerusalem. Obadiah speaks of God's promise to judge Edom and to restore His people.

Jonah (pronounced joe-nuh)

Jonah is the story of a prophet who doesn't want to obey God. When he is told to warn the people in a wicked city that God is about to destroy them, he tries to run away from God. He happens to believe this particular city (Ninevah) really deserves to be destroyed; after all, it is the capital of Israel's enemy, Assyria. But God isn't interested in our opinions, and He also doesn't appreciate disobedience – something Jonah has to learn the hard way.

Micah (pronounced mike-uh)

Writing more than a century before the overthrow of Jerusalem, Micah uses a poetic style to call the people to repentance for their sinful activities. As with so many Old Testament prophets, God inspires Micah to speak a combination of warning and hope, including some very specific promises about the King who will one day rule God's people perfectly.

Nahum (pronounced nay-hum)

Nahum, like Jonah, prophesies against the Assyrian capital of Nineveh. This time, however, it isn't a matter of warning them, for God has definitely decided to destroy them. Nahum's words are partly to encourage the people of Judah (who are very fearful after

Assyria's capture of Israel) and partly to emphasize God's displeasure with all sin, including their own.

Habakkuk (pronounced huh-back-uk)

Habakkuk wrote just before Judah was captured by the Babylonians. This book contains a question and answer session between the prophet and God. Habakkuk asks God how long the current chaos is going to last. God's answer: You haven't seen anything yet. Question two: Why are you letting wicked people get away with what they do? God's answer: I won't, just wait. The prophet finally responds with a prayer that speaks of his hope in God, no matter what this life brings.

Zephaniah (pronounced zef-uh-nye-uh)

Zephaniah also wrote his book before Judah was captured. He happened to live during one of the few times when Judah was ruled by a righteous king, Josiah. During these years the people begin to feel safe, and as a result become careless in their obedience to and respect for God. Zephaniah's words come thundering into this season of false peace with some very frightening warnings.

Haggai (pronounced hag-eye or hag-ee-eye)

Moving forward again in history, Haggai is among the exiles who are allowed to return to Jerusalem to rebuild the temple. His writings deal with some problems that arise during this rebuilding process. For one thing, the people have gotten distracted by building their own houses. They have also become discouraged because the new temple is not as wonderful as the original one was and God's presence does not seem as near. Haggai's assignment is to bring them back on track, and to assure them that God's glory will one day return even more powerfully than before.

Zechariah (pronounced zeck-uh-rye-uh)

Zechariah begins his writings only months after Haggai completed his. Opening with a warning to obey God, Zechariah then records a series of eight visions he has received from God. He helpfully explains what each vision means to the people of Judah, usually something very encouraging. The rest of this book paints a broad picture of Judah's story, beginning with their recent captivity and sweeping ahead to the first and the second comings of their Messiah. It speaks of both the great sufferings and the wonderful redemption God's people will experience.

Malachi (pronounced mal-uh-kye)

Even after the lessons they should have learned from their Babylonian captivity, most of Judah still does not live in obedience to God. In this closing book of the Old Testament, God makes it very clear through the words of His prophet that He is not pleased with the corruption He sees, both in the people themselves and in the priests He has placed over them. He promises to send a "Messenger" (His Son) to purify the land, and it won't be a pleasant process. But for those who remain faithful to Him, it will eventually result in great healing and joy.

The Years between the Old and New Testaments

After many generations of fairly steady communication from God to His people, there is a period of silence that lasts approximately four hundred years. During this time Judah comes to be controlled by two significant conquerors. The first is Alexander the Great. During his rule Greek becomes the official language of the region. Years later, Rome makes the land of Israel part of their massive empire, and they are still in charge when Jesus comes to earth. Among other things they build an extensive system of roads that will eventually allow the early Christian believers to spread the gospel more easily.

The New Testament Books

Matthew

God wisely tells us about Jesus' life on earth, including His death and resurrection, from four different perspectives. You will find in each of the gospels a mix of stories, conversations, and teachings, along with comments from the writers that help to explain or put things into context. Matthew is particularly interested in Jesus' place in Jewish history. He quotes Old Testament writers over forty times, demonstrating that Jesus is in fact the Messiah about whom they were writing. You will also find lots of interactions between Jesus and the Pharisees. These men are the authorities in the Jewish church, but they do not understand who Jesus is and therefore fiercely resent His popularity and teachings.

Mark

Mark's gospel is the easiest to read and is sometimes recommended as a good starting point for Bible beginners. He moves fairly rapidly from one scene in Jesus' life to the next, and is careful to make things clear for readers who might not understand the Jewish culture. He calls our attention to the suffering of Christ, but he also points out the authority Jesus has over nature, sickness, demons, and death itself. In Mark, as in all the gospels, you will find a number of 'parables,' which are images and stories Jesus uses to clarify important lessons about how the kingdom of God operates.

Luke

Luke is a doctor, and like any good physician he pays close attention to details. His goal, he tells us, is to give an "orderly account" of the life of Jesus, so history will have a thorough and accurate record of what really happened during the thirty-three years when God walked the earth as a man. Luke spends more time than the other gospel writers on the events of Jesus' birth, and provides careful descriptions of many of the miracles He performs. You will also get frequent glimpses into Jesus' relationship with the twelve men who are His disciples (specially chosen followers).

John

John, Peter, and James were Jesus' three closest friends, and therefore they knew Him better than anyone else. You will find John's writings to be deeply theological, rather than simply descriptive. While this can sometimes make them harder to understand, you will also discover in them rich and wonderful truths about God and His design for the world. John wants you to know about God's love, His power, and His holiness. For this reason he shares some of the most personal conversations Jesus had with His disciples and with other individuals. As you read through this book, you will get a sense of who Jesus is as a human and as God, and you will also learn about both the hardships and the rewards that are promised to those who choose to follow Him.

Acts

This book, also called the Acts of the Apostles, was written by Dr. Luke as a sequel to his gospel. It picks up with the story of the early church that is formed after Jesus rose from the dead and returned to heaven. At first most of the people who believe in Christ live in Jerusalem, but soon they begin to be persecuted and even killed, and so they (and their gospel message) start to spread into many other regions. The early part of Acts tells of the teachings and miracles being performed by the apostles such as Peter and John. But soon it switches to the story of a man named Paul, who (once God gets his attention) becomes a great missionary to the Gentiles (people who are not Jews), and who is responsible for starting new churches in many lands. When he is eventually put in prison, he writes letters to these and other churches, letters which make up much of the remainder of the New Testament.

Romans

Paul's letter to the Romans is not the first letter he wrote, but the men who put the Bible together probably made it first because it contains a thorough and systematic explanation of the truths of salvation. Paul has actually not yet been in Rome himself at this point, so he wants to make Christianity as clear as possible to the new believers who live there. His discussion of our fallenness, our desperate need for God's redemption, and the supernatural life God now offers is the best in all of scripture. As you read through Romans, try to sort between the things only God can do and the things we who have received His grace are required to do in order to stay strong in our faith.

I Corinthians

Paul seems to have a particularly deep concern for the Christians in Corinth, a city in southern Greece where he had started a church. Because they live in a very pagan culture, the young congregation struggles with a lot of temptations and confusions that pastor Paul must deal with, sometimes rather drastically. As a result, churches down through history can now read his detailed instructions on such matters as church discipline, spiritual immaturity, sexual relationships and roles, guidelines for church services, and the proper use of supernatural gifts.

II Corinthians

While there is evidence that Paul wrote a number of letters to the Corinthian church, these two are the only ones we have. This letter is more personal and emotional than I Corinthians. Paul speaks of suffering (including his own) not only as something Christians should expect, but also as something that is intended by God to accomplish good things in our lives. He calls the church to repentance, to holiness, to generosity, and to faithfulness to each other and to the truths of God. We also learn more about Paul as a person in this book than in any of his other letters.

Galatians

Galatia was not a city, but rather a region in Asia, so this letter is actually addressed to a number of churches in that area. In this letter Paul deals with a very specific deception these churches are facing. Certain Jewish teachers have begun to tell them that in order to be a Christian, they must practice all the Jewish customs as well. Paul begins his argument by explaining why he is qualified to make a decision regarding this matter. He then explains how faith in Christ is the only path to God, and why Jesus' sacrifice fulfilled all of God's requirements for salvation.

Ephesians

Paul once spent two full years in Ephesus, where he developed a very close friendship with this group of believers. He writes this letter to the Ephesians after he becomes a prisoner in Rome. The focus of this wonderful book is not the people or their problems, but God Himself. Paul deeply desires the church to know God in the fulness of His glory and to become His representatives on earth in such a way that others will understand His nature and purposes. He finishes the letter with a reminder that Christians must do battle with our enemy, the devil, taking care that we ourselves are continually clothed in righteousness and armed with faith and truth.

Philippians

Although this letter to the church in Philippi is also written during Paul's imprisonment, it is a letter full of joy and love. The Philippians have just sent a generous gift to support him. Paul wants to thank them and to let them to know that God is also blessing him in many other ways during this season of his life. He encourages them to follow the model of Jesus, who humbled Himself by coming to earth to die, and he challenges them to walk in purity without complaining, so the world will see God's beauty through their lives.

Colossians

Colosse was a tiny community in Asia that Paul never visited. The leader of the church had apparently contacted him concerning some false teachings that were influencing the Colossians. This error claimed that Jesus was just one of a number of people who had somehow reached a god-like status. Paul is very emphatic that Jesus alone is fully God and fully man, that He is God's eternal Son, and that He is the Savior of and sovereign Lord over His church. He also warns the church to watch out for any kind of false ideas, unnecessary rules, or worldly habits that would draw them away from their faith.

I Thessalonians

Located on a busy harbor in northern Greece, Thessalonica was also the capital of a Roman province. Paul's message of salvation through Christ won the hearts of many people there, but it angered the Jewish and Roman leaders. After he left, Paul sent his co-worker Timothy back to check on the young church. When he receives word that they are doing well, he writes this letter expressing his relief and gratitude. He also takes the opportunity to speak of what will happen at the end of human history, when Christ will come to earth for the second time to rescue His church before the sinful world is destroyed.

II Thessalonians

This second letter continues the theme of end-time judgments. Apparently the people in Thessalonica thought this time would come very soon, and some of them had even stopped working. To clarify things, Paul tells them of certain events that must take place before the "day of the Lord," including the rise of a false leader who will deceive many with his supernatural abilities. Paul emphasizes the importance of staying faithful to the truths they have been taught, so they won't be misled by these powerful deceptions.

I Timothy

Besides his letters to churches, the Bible also contains several letters Paul wrote to individuals. Timothy was a young believer whose mother was Jewish but whose father was Greek. For a while Timothy traveled with Paul and helped with his ministry, but eventually Paul left him to oversee the church in Ephesus. This letter gives Timothy guidance on how to lead the church, and how to select other leaders. It is filled with specific, practical wisdom.

II Timothy

Paul's second letter to Timothy was written several years later. Aware that he does not have long to live, Paul urges Timothy to come visit him. He writes with the emotion of a loving father who wants to encourage his son to be strong and to carry on well, even after his mentor is gone. He warns Timothy that there will be persecutions, not only in his own lifetime, but especially when the end-time draws near. Again Paul points to the truths of scripture as the only place of safety and strength.

Titus

Titus was another young man mentored by Paul, who was later appointed to care for a church on the island of Crete. This church was having relationship difficulties, so Paul spells out for Titus the proper behaviors not only of church leaders, but also of the godly men and women in the church. He encourages them to live righteously, keeping their thoughts focused on the eventual return of Christ.

Philemon

The story behind this little letter is that Philemon, in whose house the Colossian church meets, has a runaway slave who has ended up in Rome. There this slave, Onesimus, meets Paul and accepts Jesus as his savior. Now that the slave and his former master have become brothers in Christ, Paul writes Philemon to encourage their reconciliation. Paul also promises to pay for any debts Onesimus owes to Philemon.

Hebrews

This grand letter is the Bible's mystery book. It is possible that Paul wrote it, but there is no proof, and in many ways it is very different from his other letters. There are words and ideas in this book that appear nowhere else in scripture. Because it is written to the Hebrews (another name for Jews), it focuses on questions they might have. After depending on obedience to the law for nearly fifteen hundred years, the Jewish people have a hard time accepting the free gift of salvation. The author of Hebrews discusses the history of the priesthood and the covenants, explaining that they were models for what God has now accomplished through Jesus Christ. He then gives them (and us) a marvelous sermon on the power of faith.

James

The final series of New Testament letters are named for the men who wrote them, rather than for the people to whom they were written. James was a common name in Bible days, so we can't be sure of the author of this book. Traditionally it is thought to be Jesus' brother who became a leader in the early church in Jerusalem. James' letter is a favorite of many Bible readers, simply because it is so clear and direct and practical. He focuses not on the "talk" of Christianity, but on the "walk." We might put a warning sign on this book: No hypocrites allowed!

I Peter

As we mentioned earlier, Peter was one of Jesus' three closest disciples. Many people who read about him in the gospels can identify with his impulsive, even reckless personality. But over the years Peter came to a deep understanding not only of the power and holiness of Jesus, but also of the necessity and value of suffering. In this letter he shares his wisdom with the churches of his day, who also face severe persecution. He encourages them to live as though this earth is not their home, keeping their minds and hearts centered on pleasing their Lord. He also provides some specific instructions regarding personal behaviors, including marriage and church relationships.

II Peter

This letter was written a number of years later, shortly before Peter was put to death by the Romans. This time he is concerned about the false teachings that are already misleading many believers. He warns the church that intellectual knowledge about God is not enough. Instead, the knowledge God gives is supernatural and life-changing, producing godly fruit that is visible to others. Peter also makes a powerful comparison between the trustworthy teachings of scripture and the deceptive doctrines of false prophets and teachers.

I, II and III John

The three letters of the apostle John, one longer, the others quite short, reveal his fatherly concern to minister truth to those who are followers of Jesus. He apparently is very aware of some important errors that are seeping into their thinking. He understands the vital need for each believer to know God intimately by having an authentic personal experience of His love, His forgiveness, and His ongoing faithfulness. John explains that God's love is sacrificial, and he calls the church to demonstrate that same kind of love. He also warns them to watch for false spirits that will claim to be from God, but which will lead them away from Christ.

Jude

Like James, Jude may have been another brother of Jesus and also a leader in the Jerusalem church. Once again, the motivation for his letter is the existence of damaging distortions that are making their way into the Christian churches. He warns that the false teachers will appear to have supernatural wisdom and authority, but will give themselves away by their lack of understanding of God's holiness and sovereignty. He calls on believers to rely on God's Spirit and His scriptures for their nourishment and direction.

Revelation

The Bible concludes with the lengthy account of a vast and terrifying vision that was given to the apostle John, who had been exiled by the Romans onto a tiny island called Patmos. In his vision Jesus appears to him, not as the earthly friend and teacher with whom he once walked, but as the almighty Lord of creation and judgment. Jesus commands John to write what he sees. He then shows John a series of dramatic events, often containing mysterious symbols, that represent the coming tribulations of the church and the eventual conclusion of human history on earth.

As you read through this powerful book, some parts will be very clear, while other portions will be impossible to understand. Scholars over the centuries have pondered the meaning of what God chose to reveal to John. But there is no denying that He intended this revelation to produce overwhelming fear in our hearts, a fear that should put into clear perspective every aspect of our lives.

Unless the one true God – who long ago called creation into existence and who will one day return it to dust and ashes – unless He has truly chosen to redeem those who will receive Him as Lord, we have no hope whatsoever.

But that very redemption is the story and the glory of scripture. And that is what I pray you will discover and embrace, as you make your way into the pages of these ancient and eternal writings.

PART THREE

Going Further

Studying a Sample Chapter

Now that you have a much better idea of the contents of your Bible, I'd like to use this final section to discuss a couple different ways to approach Bible study. Basically, you can either concentrate on the details of scripture by digging down into a particular passage, or you can back away and look for ideas and lessons that can be drawn from the Bible as a whole.

I've selected the first chapter of the book of Psalms as a good place to show you how to take an "up-close" look at a particular scripture. I'm going to be using the translation of the Bible I personally prefer, the New King James Version. If you have a different translation the verses won't be exactly the same, but they should have the same meaning.

Before we begin, I should point out that the chapters in Psalms were actually written separately from each other. In other words, each chapter is a complete unit. In the rest of the Bible, chapter divisions were put in later to make the books easier to read. Therefore when you're studying anything besides Psalms, be sure to look at the verses before and after each chapter, in case they have something important to add.

Oh, by the way, there's no rule that says you have

to study one chapter at a time. Sometimes you'll want to examine two or three chapters at once, while other times you'll find rich treasures in only a few verses. Also remember that because there are many kinds of writings in the Bible, not all of them will contain a lesson on God's ways as directly as this psalm does.

Okay, let's see what we can learn from Psalm 1.

Step One – Read it!

Blessed is the man
Who walks not in the counsel of the ungodly,
Nor stands in the path of sinners,
Nor sits in the seat of the scornful;
But his delight is in the law of the Lord,
And in His law he meditates day and night.
He shall be like a tree
Planted by the rivers of water,
That brings forth its fruit in its season,
Whose leaf also shall not wither;
And whatever he does shall prosper.
The ungodly are not so,
But are like the chaff which the wind drives away.
Therefore the ungodly shall not stand in the judgment,
Nor sinners in the congregation of the righteous.
For the Lord knows the way of the righteous,
But the way of the ungodly shall perish.

Step Two – Figure out the basic idea

The most obvious thing about this psalm is that it compares two people, or two kinds of people: the righteous and the ungodly. It also describes two things about them: how they behave, and what will happen to them. If you were to make a simple outline, it might look like this:

I. Righteous man
    A. Doesn't hang out with the ungodly
    B. Spends his time thinking about the laws of God
    C. Is blessed and will grow and prosper

II. Ungodly man
    A. Gets blown around
    B. Won't be in the group of the righteous on judgment day
    C. Will perish

Step Three – Research

Sometimes you won't want or need to take this step as you're reading through a passage. But often it can be quite helpful.

1. *Definitions.*
No question about it, it's hard to understand anything you read if you don't know what all the words mean. Let's say you aren't sure about two of the words

in Psalm 1, "meditate" and "chaff."

A dictionary will tell you that "meditate" means to think carefully about or to ponder something. That's what you're doing here! "Chaff" is the outer shell of a grain that has to be removed before the grain can be ground into flour.

You will also find that a Bible dictionary can some-times give you greater insight. If you look up "chaff" there, you will probably learn that in Bible times grains were poured onto a hard surface and beaten with sticks. They were then thrown into the air so the wind could blow away the light chaff, leaving the solid grain to fall to the ground.

2. *Bible notes.*

If your Bible has notes, often there are things you can learn from them as well. However, always remem-ber that these notes are human ideas, and should be kept separate from God's ideas in the verses. In other words, they could be wrong. Notes may tell you details about these verses that come from other historical writings or other parts of the Bible, they can explain terms, and they can help you think about what the verses are teaching.

In my Bible, for example, there is a note that says the Hebrew word translated "law," *torah*, refers to more than just what we might consider to be legal matters, but actually includes all the instructions of God.

3. *Cross references.*

While these are also put there by human writers, they connect us with something else God has written, and are therefore more reliable. One cross reference in my Bible's margin connects the word "prosper" to Psalm 128. If you turn there, you will discover something about God's idea of prosperity.

Blessed is every one who fears the Lord,
who walks in His ways.
When you eat the labor of your hands,
You shall be happy, and it shall be well with you.
Your wife shall be like a fruitful vine
In the very heart of your house,
Your children like olive plants
All around your table.
Behold, thus shall the man be blessed
Who fears the Lord.
The Lord bless you out of Zion,
And may you see the good of Jerusalem
All the days of your life.
Yes, may you see your children's children.
Peace be upon Israel!

From this psalm you learn that God's blessings can be very real and practical, and can especially include a healthy, peaceful, stable family life.

Step Four – Go a little deeper

Returning to Psalm 1, we need to spell out in more detail the choices that lead to these blessings and prosperity for the righteous man. First, he does not walk in the counsel of ungodly men. That simply means he doesn't listen to their wisdom, or do things the way they recommend. He also doesn't "stand in their paths" or "sit in their seats." This probably means he doesn't join them in their activities.

Instead, he is so busy meditating on the teachings of God "day and night" that they have actually become delightful to him. No longer is he attracted to the things that delight the world, which would draw him onto the pathway of worldly amusements, or which would tempt him to join ungodly men in scorning and making jokes about others.

The result of these godly choices is pictured as being like a tree that has its roots close to a running river. With a constant supply of water being drawn up into it, the tree bears its fruit right on time, and its leaves are always green and strong. In the same way, the flowing river of God's wisdom results in the prosperity He has intended for this man to enjoy.

By contrast, the ungodly man is dry and useless, like chaff in the wind. The psalmist also warns that he will not be included with the righteous in the day when God judges every man. For you see, the ultimate prosperity God offers us will be received not on this earth but in heaven, and will last for all eternity.

Step Five – Applying God's truth to our lives

No matter what you're reading, it is always wise to ask God to show you what He might want you to learn personally about His principles, His personality, and His plans. In the case of Psalm 1, what can we discover?

For one thing, we learn that God divides people into two groups: those who are godly, that is, those who are like Him, and those who aren't. You will actually find this division over and over again throughout scripture. What you won't ever find is a third group, people who are half-and-half. People are either delighted by the things the world finds attractive, or they are delighted by God Himself.

We are also told that God "knows the way of the righteous." Another way to say this is that He is familiar with their way because it is His way as well. Moreover, His way is prosperous. By contrast, the way of the ungodly will be destroyed.

Probably the most important lesson from this psalm, however, and one that God intends each of us who reads it to contemplate, is that our eternal destiny is going to be the result of our own daily choices. It's much more than a one-time prayer we pray or even certain religious actions we perform.

Rather, our righteousness (or our ungodliness) will be the result of our "day and night" thoughts and associations. It has to do with where we walk, where we stand, and where we sit. The healthy tree planted by the river drinks continually of its waters. The chaff gets blown away without a second chance.

And so, my friend, please tuck these verses into your heart, and begin your meditations with them. Allow them to gradually replace the noise and confusion of so much of what the world has taught you. God's truths are simple, deep, eternal, and life-giving. You may never have thought His thoughts or walked in His ways before, but as you begin to, you will discover that they bring a wonderful and powerful nourishment to your inner soul. As you drink in His wisdom and understanding, God will remove the loneliness, brokenness, fear, and despair that has piled up over the years, and will fill you instead with His joy, His peace, His strength, and His love.

Taking in the Big Picture

The final thing we need to discuss is how to view the Bible as a whole unit. As the months go by and you are faithful in your studies, you will begin to discover clear patterns of thought that weave their way throughout the entire scriptures like threads through a piece of cloth. You will also begin to identify God's unchanging principles that appear consistently within the Bible writings.

If you wish, however, you can speed up this process of discovery by deliberately researching certain topics. One excellent way to do this is by using your concordance. As we explained earlier, a concordance is a listing of verses that contain certain words. If your Bible doesn't have a concordance, they are also published as separate books or as computer programs.

Think of a particular subject that interests you or a question you would like to have answered. For example, you might want to know what the Bible teaches about raising children, or God's perspective on anger and forgiveness, or what can be learned about angels and demons. For a more complete study, you should not only check the exact words (like "angels" and "demons"), but also other related words.

Let's say you want to find the biblical view of

money and wealth. In that case you could look in your concordance for "money," "riches," "coins," "wages," and "debt." You would create a list of verses containing these words, and then find them in your Bible. Whenever you discover a passage that is especially helpful, be sure to check for cross references in your Bible's margins. Some Bibles also include topical studies as part of their notes. These are likely to address some of your questions, and may even give you ideas for other subjects to research.

You should also watch for subjects that God Himself must consider especially important, simply because they show up often. For example, scriptures frequently mention such topics as the nature of faith, the kingdom of God, and the consequences of sin. Sometimes you'll find direct teachings on these subjects, but just as often the lessons are built into the stories themselves. Part of becoming a mature Christian is the deliberate training of our perspective to match God's point of view. The best way for this to happen is through thoughtfully reading (and systematically memorizing) scripture.

Another good habit is to pay attention to the prayers people pray, and consider how God responds to them. Remember, even though Bible characters lived a long time ago in a very different culture, they were still just human beings like ourselves. They had the same fears, the same doubts, the same confusions, and the same need for God's wisdom and help. We can learn to pray in the manner that pleases God by seeing how He answers prayers in the Bible.

A somewhat different type of "thread" you can contemplate as you read through your Bible concerns the prophecies of scripture. It can be very interesting to compare the predictions in the Old Testament to their fulfillment in later years. Usually these connections are noted in the cross references, making it easy for you to identify them.

If this kind of study particularly intrigues you, there are also many books written by people who have spent years examining biblical prophecy. Some researchers work very hard trying to figure out which prophecies and promises may come to pass in our own lifetime. Even though the Bible stopped being written nearly two thousand years ago, God certainly hasn't stopped working out His plans in the years since.

Never forget, though, that God does not intend everything in His word to be perfectly clear to us. While some prophecies are specific and easy to understand, most of them only give us hints and pieces of ideas, and often contain strange symbols or descriptions of events and places whose meanings we can only guess. Therefore it is wise to read a number of interpretations of prophecy, always praying that God Himself will help you sort out what is true, and even more, that He will reveal to you which prophecies should make a difference in your life.

As you become more and more familiar with scripture, you will eventually encounter some other questions (besides the interpretation of prophecy) that have puzzled Bible readers for many years. In particular, there are several strong threads of thought that show up in scripture which seem to directly contradict each other.

One of these mysteries is the question of whether God controls everything, or whether we are free to make our own decisions. Both ideas can be found in a number of places in the Bible. For example, in Proverbs 21:1 we read, "The king's heart is in the hand of the Lord, like the rivers of water; He turns it wherever He wishes." That certainly sounds like God is in control. Yet in I Kings 11:11 we find God holding King Solomon personally responsible for the bad choices he made. "Because you...have not kept My covenant and My statutes, which I have commanded you, I will surely tear the kingdom away from you and give it to your servant."

Our human logic cannot understand how the same decision can be controlled by two separate beings. If God is truly directing our hearts and our choices, how does He then hold us accountable for what we decide to do? Some Christians have resolved this question by believing there is no such thing as free will. Others have taken the view that God doesn't really control everything.

But there is a third consideration to take into account, which is that this confusion could actually be the result of the limits of human logic. One principle the Bible clearly teaches is that we humans do not, and cannot, understand everything. Here is what God spoke through the prophet Isaiah, in Isaiah 55:8-9:

"For My thoughts are not your thoughts,
Nor are your ways My ways," says the Lord.
"For as the heavens are higher than the earth,
So are My ways higher than your ways,
And My thoughts than your thoughts."

He also makes a similar statement through Paul (Romans 11:33-34):

Oh, the depth of the riches both of the wisdom and knowledge of God!
How unsearchable are His judgments and His ways past finding out!
"For who has known the mind of the Lord?
Or who has become His counselor?"

It appears that God's logic can definitely be different, and "higher," than ours. Why would He do this? Well, He understands that part of making Him Lord of our lives requires a willingness to trust Him even when we don't understand how He thinks. Our pride can demand that He adjust to what seems sensible and right to us. But that's getting things backwards. After all, He is God and we are not.

So in the lived-out reality of our existence, we who are followers of Christ do not have to worry about our circumstances, for we are certain that God somehow has full authority over everything in our lives. At the same time it is also our responsibility to carefully make those choices we know will please our Lord. Even though we don't exactly understand how this all works, it is completely possible to do both things. We can in fact trust and obey.

■ ■ ■ ■ ■

Hopefully you will spend the rest of your life tracing these various themes throughout the Bible, wrestling with the questions, yet delighting in the beauty and comfort of God's truths. Nevertheless, the most important message by far in all of scripture is God's amazing plan for the redemption of His people. You will find it showing up from the beginning of the Bible to the very end. For this reason I have chosen to conclude this book by putting into my own words what I have learned, through decades of scripture study, about the greatest story ever told.

Conclusion – The Gospel Story

In the beginning of time, God created humans to be very much like Himself, able to enjoy the wonders of the natural universe, but also able to have a deep and amazing relationship with each other and with their Creator. For some reason we don't entirely understand, the first humans, Adam and Eve, were not satisfied with all God had given them, and chose to take for themselves the one thing He had held back.

This simple act of rebellion broke everything. It caused creation to become filled with violence, destruction and death. It caused Adam and Eve (and their children after them) to become corrupted with shame, anger, bitterness and pride. Worst of all, it meant they could no longer be close to God. God, you see, is completely holy, and nothing that is corrupt can get near Him.

Yet in His great mercy, God did not abandon or destroy His creation nor the humans He loved. As you will read in the Old Testament stories, He communicated to them through His prophets, and performed many miracles on their behalf. Always His desire was for them to seek Him and to obey His laws.

But because sin was so deeply a part of them, their seeking and the obedience they attempted never lasted long. Generation after generation followed in the steps of Adam and Eve, always desiring that which was not theirs to have.

Yet even before Adam and Eve rebelled, God had prepared a plan to restore the humans He had made back to perfection. It was an enormously expensive plan, the most costly thing that could ever be imagined. That's because there was someone who was even more precious to Him than the human race: His only son Jesus.

Think about it. Suppose someone asked you to give up your life for something very important. It would be hard. You might not be willing to do it, but just maybe you would. Now suppose that, instead of *you* dying, you were asked to give up the life of your only child for this important cause. That would be very, very much harder.

But God did something even more difficult than this. Not only did He give His son to die, but the Bible also tells us (in Isaiah 53) that He personally put His son to death. And it wasn't a quick death either. It was a long, slow, torturous, awful death.

Yet Jesus Himself was also willing for this plan to take place. From His side, He had to leave the perfection of heaven and come into our dirty, painful, nasty world as a human being, a man who experienced temptation and fatigue and rejection in the same way we do. He also had to say yes to what He knew would be one of the most painful ways to die humans have ever invented.

Plus, Jesus had to do something we will never

understand. He had to supernaturally take into His perfect, sinless soul all the evil things that have ever been thought or said or done by all humans throughout all of history. It was an unthinkably hideous and bitter burden.

But there, on a barren hill outside the walls of Jerusalem, a history-shattering miracle took place. When this Man who Himself had committed no sins willingly offered Himself in our place, and when His righteous, holy Father accepted that sacrifice, the love this represented reversed the curse that had come upon Adam and Eve, and freed creation from the consequences of sin. But it didn't stop there. On the third day, death gave up its power over Him, the Spirit of God breathed life back into Him, and Jesus Christ arose from the grave as conqueror and king.

Think about what this means. Because He took our sin, He is now able to give us *His* righteousness. Because Jesus was willing to be separated from His Father, we can now be reunited with Him. Because He was willing to die the death we deserved, we have been given the opportunity to receive His eternal life.

All that remains is for each of us to open ourselves to His gift. We must ask His Spirit to give us eyes to see ourselves as He does, and the grace to believe what He has done for us. We must allow Him to probe deeply into the corners of our minds and hearts, searching out the hidden doubts and fears and sins, bringing us to an understanding of the hopelessness of our own efforts and our lostness apart from His mercy.

But once we are able to make the transaction,

deliberately laying down every desire we have except the desire to know Him, we will find ourselves being filled with the newness of His life. We will feel the heavy weight of our own guilt being lifted by the power of His forgiveness. We will come to understand that our lives have purpose, that there are specific assignments we were created to accomplish. We will begin to discover a wonderful new family of other believers who have also found Him.

What's more, we will learn to view this present life as nothing but a temporary season during which we are privileged to serve our Lord, but which will soon pass away and be replaced by a life so glorious that we will wonder why we ever valued anything else. And above all, we will be filled with deep thankfulness and love for the God who has loved us with a love that goes beyond all understanding.

Now at last, dear reader, it's time to lay this little book aside, and pick up your Bible. Open it with gratitude, with curiosity, with expectation, and with humility, knowing that the Creator of the universe and the Savior of our souls is eager to meet you on those pages.